**Also by Laura J. Kendall:**


**12 Steps to your Inner Sex Goddess**

**How to Write~A Daring Writer's Handbook**

**A Simple Case of Suicide**

**A Simple Case of Revenge**

**Witches Enchantment**

**The Top Five 911 Emergencies and How to Handle Them Until the Paramedics Arrive!**

**The Top Five Winter Emergencies and How to Handle Them Until the Paramedics Arrive!**

# How to Write:

# A Daring Writer's Workbook

*By Laura J. Kendall, CPC*

*For everyone who dares to write!*

This workbook is intended for informational purposes only. **The information is current at the time of publication.** The author and publisher assume no liability for omissions, errors, or outcomes. Completing this workbook does not guarantee specific results or outcomes.

*Publishing Division of LJ Kendall Coaching & Training Solutions, LLC*

Dedicated to all who dare to write. Writing opens up the soul and exposes the author to gentle release or harsh critique. For this I honor you!

# How to Write:

# A Daring Writer's Workbook

# SUCCESS STORIES

A few years ago, it was unheard of for a self-published writer to become a successful, mainstream author.

Well hold onto your hat because times have changed! Thanks to computers and the Internet, many self-published writers are becoming huge, and sometimes overnight, successes.

A recent success story is that of writer EL James, who self published a little book you may have heard of—"Fifty Shades of Grey." The novel has been picked up by a major publisher for seven figures and James is now a reputable mainstream author.

Amanda Hockings, a paranormal fiction writer, is another great success story. Hockings wrote several novels over nine years, all of which were rejected by publishers.  One April day in 2010 she decided on a whim to digitally upload her books on amazon.com. Within six months she sold 150,000 copies of her books. Her books sales are now in the millions and growing right along with her bank account, and she did it all without the help of an agent or publishing house.

Michael Prescott had gained recognition, success, and critical praise for twenty books he wrote over thirty years. Then came the overwhelming rejection by agents and publishers of his latest thriller, "Riptide." Prescott thought for sure his dreams, career, and success were over. Then he decided to self publish "Riptide" as an eBook. He priced it at 99 cents and sold over 800,000 digital copies!

They are among many self-published authors successfully selling their books as eBooks. Today authors can take control of their careers through self publishing. Many get noticed by big publishing houses and are offered lucrative deals. Self publishing is no longer frowned upon, and many successful writers are being discovered this way.

I began self publishing using a great company called Infinity Publishing, and more recently I've published using Create Space (owned by Amazon). I've enjoyed Create Space and have found the support team to be fantastic.

I've doubled my profits by offering my books in paperback and eBook format.

To date, I have self published three full-length novels, two first aid books, the companion handbook to this workbook and my newest book - 12 Steps to your Inner Sex Goddess. If I can do it, so can you!

# ARE YOU A DARING WRITER?

To become a published writer, you must have a compelling reason to take this journey.

Why do you want to write a book?

What actions are you willing to take to make it happen?

What might be getting in the way?

Writing can be frustrating and lonely at times. To write a book is to decide against all odds that you will complete it and publish it!

What is your reason for writing your book? Is it to:

See your name on the cover?

Be a published author?

Create a family heirloom for future generations?

Create an ultimate business card that you will give to prospective clients?

Have your book go viral and become an instant overnight sensation and millionaire?

See the story that has been swirling around in your mind, finally down on paper?

These are just a few examples of compelling reasons to write a book.

Why do you want to write a book? Write it down! Own it! Once you do, nothing and no one will stop you from achieving it!

There will be many well-meaning and some not-so-well meaning people along your journey. Stay true to yourself and follow your heart, not the opinions of others.

Surround yourself with people who support you and your dream. Keep these gems close. Remember, when others put you down or mock you, it is never about you; it is always about them and their insecurities, self doubt, self hate or jealousy. They are the ones who have no vision.

*"You have to believe in yourself when no one else does. That's what makes you a winner." Venus Williams*

# State Your Compelling Reason

**The top three reasons I want to write a book are:**

**1.**

**2.**

**3.**

**From your list, what is your top reason for writing your book? A reason that is so compelling that nothing will stop you! Write it below.**

**MY COMPELLING REASON:**

# What is stopping you?

Now that you have your compelling reason, let's look at what might be stopping you from following through.

The top three reasons I haven't followed through writing my book are:

1.

2.

3.

We all have things that get in the way of following through or believing in ourselves. Mine was my huge inner critic known as the "I'm-not-good-enough gremlin." I let this belief infiltrate every aspect of my life. For sixteen years my inner critic prevented me from writing my first book.

Once you face your own gremlin or inner critic, you can deal with it so it doesn't control your life. I've found that having a coach is one of the most powerful gifts I've ever given myself. Through coaching I have made amazing, positive changes, which is why I went through the training and became a Certified Professional Coach. Now I am living my dream by helping writers achieve theirs—getting their books published.

# WHAT'S YOUR GENRE?

A genre is a classification of category, such as murder mystery, romance, self help, etc. Readers know what type of story to expect from your book based on the genre.

My top three genres:

1.

2.

3.

Now think about which of the genres you listed above is your absolute favorite? Why?

My favorite Genre is:

**Four of my favorite writers from my favorite genre are:**

1.

2.

3.

4.

What is it about their stories that resonates with you? How do their stories make you FEEL? What emotions do they bring out in you? Do you disappear into another world for a while?

Understanding why your favorite writers resonate so highly with you can give you great clues as to how you want your writing style to flow. I am by no means saying you should or must write like another writer. You must find your own voice and write in a way that you enjoy. When people read my books they always tell me they can hear my voice in the characters' words. I don't follow anyone else's style because my style is my own. Not everyone will like my style, and that's OK. I am proud of my books, and you should be proud of yours, too.

# WHO ARE YOUR CHARACTERS?

Protagonist - the main character of the story.

Antagonist - one or more characters who are in conflict with the protagonist.

Supporting characters - these characters add to the story line and have a relationship with the main character.

It is important to know your characters inside and out. I create individual profile sheets for all my characters so I can refer to them as I am writing to ensure consistency throughout the story.

Some questions I ask and answer are:

How old are they?

What kind of car do they drive?

What kind of job do they have?

What do they look like physically? (Height, hair color and length, etc.)

What foods do they like?

Where do they live?

What does their house look like?

What is their sexual orientation?

**What kind of pets do they have?**

**What are their pets' names?**

**These are just some sample questions for you to consider and expand on to create your own.**

**Once you know your characters and have a detailed description sheet one each one, writing a sequel or series will be a snap!**

## Worksheet - Character Profile

**Name:**

**Age:**

**Gender:**

**Height:**

**Weight:**

**Job/title:**

**Car/truck make and model:**

**Hair color and length:**

**Facial hair:**

**Pet's breed:**

**Pet's name:**

**State and town:**

**Type of house:**

**Vices:**

**Best friend:**

**Hobbies:**

**Sexual orientation:**

**Lover/s:**

**Unique traits or habits:**

**Anything else to remember?**

# VIEWPOINT

**From what viewpoint will your character(s) speak?**

**First person** - the main character will use the word "I" and see the world from his/her point of view.

**Second person** - Used mostly in self-help, do-it-yourself manuals or any book where a narrative style works best. Not used much in fiction novels.

**Third person** - the characters speak in "he" or "she" and the reader can see, hear, and feel everything the characters do.

I find it difficult to write in first person. Third person flows more naturally for me. You will discover what feels comfortable for you. It is your story, so if something isn't working change it.

## HOOK LINE:

The first line of your story must grab the reader. You want to capture the readers' attention so they want to keep reading. This is the line that makes your readers click the "buy" button. It is one of the most important sentences in your book. Take a look at the first lines of the books you most enjoy reading to get some ideas.

**The HOOK LINE of my book is:**

## SETTING:

This is where and how your story takes place.

Is your story in the country or big city?

Is there a weather event? Snow, rain, heat?

In what country is your story set? What state? Is the area wealthy, poor, or a combination?

I write where I know so my stories to date have been set in New Jersey. I am currently working on a novel set elsewhere in the country, which brings more challenges. Only you can decide how deep you want to get with geographical and setting descriptions. If you are writing about a setting you don't know much about, research it first. If I read a novel that gets the setting wrong, I am totally turned off.

## START WRITING!

Average length of a novel is between 60,000 to 120,000 words. The number of words varies depending on the genre so do your research so you know what to shoot for. If you decide to go the mainstream publishing route, know that each publishing house has specific submission requirements. Research the submission requirements before submitting your manuscript to a publisher or publishing house.

I based my full-length fiction novels on a minimum of 60,000 words. Computers make it easy to calculate word count no matter what font or format you use.

## FORMATTING

I recommend setting the formatting and font size before you start writing. Here's what I set before typing a single word:

**The size of the book.** In Word, go to page layout and click "size." A menu will appear. At the bottom click on the "paper size" option.

I use "custom" and then set the width and height. I prefer a width of 6 inches and height of 9 inches for novels.. For workbooks I use a different size. You can decide what size you prefer.

**Margins - trial and error.**

It took days of trying margin settings to find one I like. Here's what I use:

**Margins**

**Top 0.7**

**Inside 0.11**

**Gutter 0 .88**

**Bottom 0.7**

**Outside 0.8**

**Gutter position left**

**Font: Cambria (bigger font = bigger book = higher cost)**

**Font size: 12**

The margins will change depending on the width, height and number of pages.

If the book is more than 400 pages, it will impact the gutter size.

The **orientation** is portrait.

Multiple page setting is **mirror margins** and I **apply to the whole document.**

The first written page of a print book should start on the right. If the book page with print shows up on the left, simply add a blank page at the top of the document.

For **page numbering** I prefer a bottom footer with a different first page and I start my numbering at 0.

Inserting page numbering before you start your book will save you a world of trouble! I've done this step at the end of my books and it has been a nightmare,

**Justifying text**

I prefer to justify the text, which puts the copy in a block format. This can be done under the paragraph section while in the home tab.

**Line spacing** is a personal choice. For this workbook I used 1.15. I think it makes it an easier read. I do not use 2.0 or double spacing as it makes it look like the book has no substance and I am only trying to increase my page count.

Formatting a book at the beginning of the process is something that will pay off in the end. The formatting can be different for each book you write.

## My book's format is:

Width-

Height-

Top-

Inside-

Gutter-

Bottom-

Outside-

Gutter position-

Orientation-

**Multiple page settings-**

**Line spacing-**

# KEEPING TRACK OF YOUR STORY

For "A Simple Case of Suicide" I knew the beginning and end right from the start. With my other novels I had a basic idea of the plot, and the characters, I learned, had minds of their own. I would think they were going one way and wham off they went in a whole other direction. I really find this part of the writing process to be a blast as I never know quite where I'm going. I'm just along for the ride.

At the beginning of this workbook there is a **Character Profile sheet**. I do one of these on each of my characters so I can refer back to it and keep my characters real. This also helped me really get to know my characters inside and out and see them as real people. I know, scary right - smile.

I also do **outlines for each chapter** so I can make sure my story line flows and remains consistent. It is very easy to get caught up in writing and forget where you are going. In my novels I have a main plot and a subplot, so there is a ton of conflict going on and a variety of characters.

For "A Simple Case of Revenge" I had big pieces of paper tacked to my wall where I hand wrote my story outlines, chapter by chapter. This allowed me at a glance to see where I was and where I wanted to go.

Find a way that works for you to keep track of your plot and characters. I made the mistake of trying to follow famous writers and how they wrote. It took me years to find my own way, and now I stick to what feels right to me.

I think of my novels in four parts:

**Hook line:** The first line of the novel that grabs your readers and won't let go!

**Beginning:** Introducing your characters, the conflict, and plot.

**Middle:** The nuts and bolts of the novel. This is where you flesh out your characters and give life to your story line, plot, and conflicts.

**End:** The final chapter of your book. Where you wrap things up or, if it's part of a series, leave a cliff hanger.

# BRAINSTORMING

I love this part of writing! Brainstorming is a process that helps you develop your story or subject. Every book I have written has started with thinking about the story or subject and then brainstorming by writing down anything and everything that comes to mind.

For my fellow mystery/suspense/thriller writers out there, you will need to do some extra brainstorming. In this type of genre you will need to introduce some "red herrings" to throw your readers off course and clues to help them begin figuring out the mystery.

After I brainstorm on paper, I go back and see what fits. Some ideas will work and others won't.

Brainstorming is great if you are feeling anxious about where the plot is going or are experiencing writer's block. For me, brainstorming releases the pressure release and brings the fun back into the writing process.

## TITLE

Last, but not least in the writing process, you need to come up with a title for your book. This can be both fun and stressful.

A catchy title will draw an audience to your book.

To help title your book, ask yourself some questions:

What is my story about?

Are there any pieces of the plot that stick out in my mind?

What words describe my story?

Start with a working title, which is the title you refer to as you are writing. If it still resonates with you when the book is complete, keep it. If not, try another title that works better.

## The working title of my book is:

**Will your novel be a one-time story or will it be a series?**

**There are a lot of questions you need to ask yourself as you write your book. The following pages are a series of worksheets you can use to cultivate your ideas.**

**Paper size of book:**

**Fiction or nonfiction** (circle one)

**Genre:**

**Word count I am shooting for:**

**Viewpoint_ - circle one**

**First person**

**Second person**

**Third person**

**Main character** (protagonist):

**Conflict character/s** (antagonist/s):

## Supporting characters:

*Novel worksheet*

**Write a few sentences about the following. You should be able to sum up the conflict in a short paragraph.**

**The main conflict of the story is:**

**If there is a subplot (second minor story line going on throughout the book.)**

**Subplot conflict is:**

## Setting:

I love to introduce a weather aspect in my books. Every book I've ever read that has wind, rain, snow, cold or extreme heat, has added another great element of suspense in the setting.

*Graphic or not graphic?*

*Sex, bondage or making love?*

There are some other considerations to think about before writing a book. I did a lot of thinking before I wrote my books about how graphic I wanted them to be.

In the Simple Case series I let my imagination go wild. Nothing was off limits and there are graphic sex and murder scenes. When I hear that someone's mother read the book, I always think, "Yikes!" Feel comfortable with what you are writing. Once it is in print there is no going back.

# PUBLISHING YOUR BOOK

## Free Publishing Options

### The following services are free if you do the editing, formatting, and cover creation yourself:

**Paperback** - your choice of size.

**1. Create Space** - owned by Amazon.

Free, but they also offer a paid service to help with editing, formatting and cover creation.

This company also offers a way to publish to Kindle.

## eBooks

**2. KDP - Kindle - owned by Amazon.**

You must find a place to make your own e-cover if you use KDP-Kindle.  Myecovermaker is a service I have used and recommend.  There are other ecover providers so research which is best for you.

I use page breaks to start each new chapter, which works well on Kindle.

### 3. Pubit - Nook - owned by Barnes & Noble

They also do not provide a cover creator and their cover size requirement is larger than Kindle's.

**With Nook** I use section breaks rather than page breaks for a quality look. This is something unique to Nook.

### 4. Kobo writing life.

This is a new self-publishing platform. It is free and I found it easy to use. You have to make your own cover and it does not have an automatic previewer to see if your book formatted correctly. I used caliber, a free service, to view my book and check the formatting.

Again, **I use page breaks on this publishing platform.**

**I may use the following free publishing choices:**

1.

2.

3.

**To make ecovers I can use:**

1.

2.

3.

## Paid Publishing Companies

If you don't want to do the work yourself, there are print-on-demand publishing companies you can use. These companies each have their own fees and stipulations. There are many companies out there.

I highly suggest you utilize **WRITER BEWARE** to research any company you are considering. Don't become a victim of a scam.

**WRITER BEWARE:**
http://www.sfwa.org/for-authors/writer-beware/

I have used Create Space free with great success. I have not used the paid services and therefore cannot make recommendations regarding them.

1.**Create Space** is a print on-demand company that offers formatting, designing, and cover creation.

Create space also has the ability to publish your book to Kindle.

2. **Infinity Publishing** is a print-on-demand company that offers designing and cover creation, and will assist you in formatting. I have used this service and have found them to be great for new writers.

**3. Lightening Source** is another print-on-demand company that offers similar services.

**I will research the following print on demand companies.**

**1.**

**2.**

**3.**

**My research shows that the best company for me to use is**

**_____ for the following reasons:**

**1.**

**2.**

**3.**

**The cost for my book will be:**

**This cost will include the following:**

**Any other considerations:**

# HOW TO MARKET YOUR BOOK

## 1. Create a personal Facebook page.

## 2. Create Facebook fan page linked to my personal page.

## The name of my Facebook fan page is:

## 3. Create a Twitter account to let my friends and family know about my book.

## My Twitter name is:

## 4. Create a Google + page. Every time you post or plus one it shows up on Google search engines.

## My Google + page is:

## 5.  Issue a press release about me and my book.

**I have issued a press release to the following papers:**

**1.**

**2.**

**3.**

**4.**

# OTHER CONSIDERATIONS

**Local Bookstores** - It never hurts to ask your local bookstore to sell your book. Sometimes this is a losing proposition for the self-published writer, so always get a contract that stipulates the number of books they will carry and how much they will take from each sale.

**My local bookstores are:**

**Giveaways** - something you can give away for free, such as an online report, to attract people to my book.

**My ideas for giveaways are:**

**1.**

**2.**

**Advertising** - **If** you are placing an ad, make sure you know up front how much it will cost so you can plan your budget accordingly. Don't miss something in the fine print and wind up paying more than you expected. Proceed here at your own risk. For online advertising, I highly recommend you research how to set your ad budget, length of ad run, pay per click vs. pay for impression.

I have found that Facebook has limited e-mail help while Google has easy phone support by knowledgeable staff.

I will research and decide if I want to do an ad for my book.

Where I will advertise:

The costs:

My budget:

Lifetime budget of ad:

How long will the ad will run:

Don't do an online ad or print ad until you know exactly how much it will cost!!!!

## Post previews on document sharing sites:

**Scribd**

**Slide share**

## Commenting on other author's blogs

**Post comments and get your name out there and be sure to include a link in your post back to your website or sale page on Amazon/B&N.**

**I will comment on the following blogs and include a link to my book's sale page or website.**

**1.**

**2.**

**3.**

## Your own website

There are many companies that will design a website for you and the cost ranges from cheap to astronomical. I have created my own websites using Word Press with ipage as the host.

Most authors have their own website and it can be a simple one pager or a flashy site with many pages. It is your choice.

I will research the following hosts if I am using word press.

1.

2.

3.

I will research other companies/designers that can assist me or build a website.

1.

**2.**

**3.**

**4.**

By now you should have a pretty good idea of where to begin your exciting writing adventure. I hope you have enjoyed this workbook.

The only thing stopping you from being a published writer is... YOU.

Kick your inner critic to the curb and pick up that pen, pencil, or keyboard.

I believe in you and I know you can do it!

Laura J. Kendall of LJ Kendall Coaching & Training Solutions, LLC is available to mentor and coach you through your writing adventure by phone, Skype or in person.

LJ Kendall Coaching & Training Solutions is a full-service company that can handle all aspects of self-publishing your manuscript in paperback and eBook formats.

Are you a business person looking for a prospecting tool? Do you know about the author effect? Publishing a book makes you an expert in your field. At LJ Kendall Coaching & Training Solutions, we can write, compile and publish a book for you from one interview.

Please contact Laura J. Kendall at adaringwriter@gmail.com for further information or to schedule an individual or group writer's training course.

# NOTES

# NOTES

www.ingramcontent.com/pod-product-compliance
Lightning Source LLC
Chambersburg PA
CBHW082153290526

45794CB00008B/3275

9 781477 419885